water

SUBHASH VYAM
WITH
GITA WOLF

I LIVE IN A CITY NOW, BUT I COME FROM A SMALL VILLAGE.

I'm an artist, and like many people in my community, I had to move in search of work. My parents and sisters still live in the village, and I visit them often.

Ever since I moved, I have been thinking about our life in the village and life here in the city... there is a lot to be said, and I am very troubled sometimes about many things, but I didn't know where or how to begin.

Then some time ago, there was a incident in our village which gave me an idea.

So I decided to tell a story around it: it is about WATER.

THIS IS THE VILLAGE WHERE I WAS BORN.

At that time it was a cluster of houses, in the middle of forests and hills.

We were poor and worked hard, but most people didn't go hungry. We foraged in the forest, caught fish, kept cows and goats, and grew a few crops. We had enough eat, provided the harvest was good.

But we didn't have money to spend, and we lived from one day to another.

WE HAD HEARD THAT LIFE IN THE CITY WAS VERY DIFFERENT.

Everything was available there, and it was not difficult to earn money and live comfortably.

But most people didn't want to leave the village and go there. This was the life they were used to. We had to work hard, but we had space and lived closely with trees, plants, animals and birds... and I think we understood their ways.

In many respects, the old way of life was good...

EXCEPT FOR ONE IMPORTANT THING:
WATER.

It was always a struggle to get enough for our needs.

We depended on the rains to sow and harvest our crops. Without rain we didn't have enough to eat.

There was also a lake a couple of kilometers away, where people would go to fetch the water they needed to drink, cook and bathe. They shared it with each other, and with all the other creatures around.

I remember how happy l was as a child when I took our cow to bathe in the lake.

It was fed by streams from a large river that
flowed up in the hills. As long as there was
water in the lake, we could carry on. Over a
period of time, people came up with simple but
useful ways of directing the water. They dug
small canals, letting the water from the lake
flow through their fields.

Farming became easier.

BUT DURING THE SUMMER MONTHS, THE
LAKE WOULD DRY UP.

And then everyone suffered, especially the girls
and women, whose task it was to fetch water for
households.

I sometimes went with my sisters when they
set out... we would walk for hours up and down
the hillsides, searching for a little bit of water.
We didn't dare go home without at least half
a pot.

It would last us for one day, and then we would
have to start looking again.

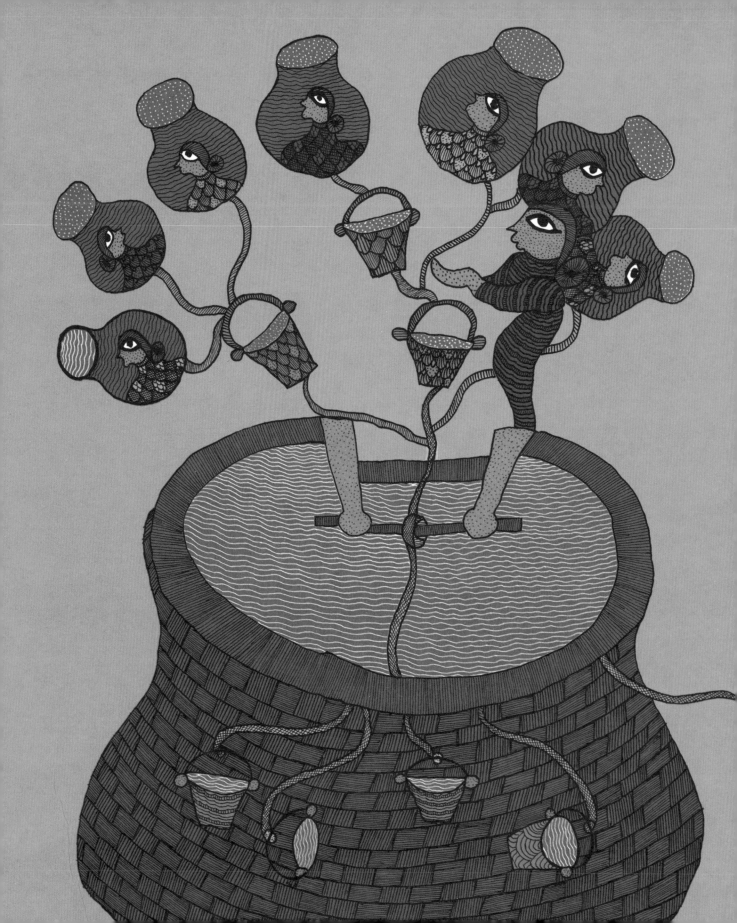

I REMEMBER WHEN THE FIRST WELL WAS
DUG IN THE VILLAGE.

It was a big moment. We were still dependent
on the rains, but at least then the wells would
fill up, and they would store water for a couple
of months.

Drawing and carrying heavy pots of water
from the well was still work that only girls and
women did. But at least now they didn't have to
walk for miles in the heat.

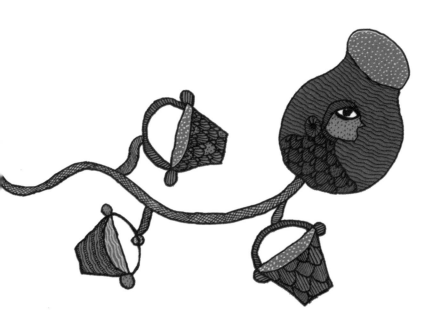

LATER, ANOTHER GREAT DEVELOPMENT CAME TO THE VILLAGE: A HAND PUMP.

It seems like a small thing now, but it was a real boon for women. We didn't have running water, but the government had dug a deep tube well, and now with a hand pump, even a small child could pump out water. It was like a miracle.

When the first pump was installed, the whole village came out to watch, and all the children lined up for a turn at it.

IT WAS AROUND THIS TIME THAT I MOVED AWAY TO A CITY TO FIND WORK.

It was a different life: it was both easier and more difficult at the same time.

I was still poor, though I earned more money.

I lived in a small flat, and missed the freedom of living in the village. The building l lived in had two huge water tanks up on the roof, and we had running water in the house, but only when the tank was full. In my neighbourhood we often went without water, although not far from us there were rich houses with lawns and swimming pools.

I discovered that you could buy water, if you had money. I never understood where this water came from, and how this was possible.

I VISITED THE VILLAGE REGULARLY TO SEE MY FAMILY.

Each time I returned, I saw a few changes.

Of course, things didn't happen as fast as they did in the city. We didn't have any powerful or rich people in the village, who could influence anything.

There were plans to run a pipeline from the lake to the village, but nothing had come of that yet.

However, a few roads and bridges appeared, and some of the houses got electricity... nothing very big, but they were welcome developments.

Still, I have to say that the wealthier families in the village benefited from these changes, while the others continued to live in the old way.

ONE DAY, MY MOTHER SENT ME A WORRIED MESSAGE TO MY FLAT IN THE CITY.

She asked me to come home right away. She seemed very worried.

It appeared that the village headman had made an announcement: she was not very clear about it, but said it had to do with water.

I discovered that there were plans to build a large dam across the river that flowed up on the hills. This was the river that fed our lake, so what would that mean for us?

NO ONE REALLY KNEW FOR SURE.

It was all everybody talked about.

The village headman said that the dam was for making electricity for the city: could that really be? Why did they want so much? It seemed greedy, without thinking about how and where it all came from.

If the river was blocked and couldn't flow, it would change its course and submerge our fields and homes. From being scarce, water would flood everything! It was a terrible thought.

Why did they want to take away what little we had? As we sat around, worried and confused, a story suddenly came into my mind. It was a tale that our mother told us as children, when my sisters and l grumbled about fetching water.

ONCE UPON A TIME, THERE WERE SEVEN SISTERS.

They were sent out by their parents to find water.

They walked all day, climbing up and down hills... until finally, they saw a lake.

But it lay deep down below, and there was no way for them to reach the water.

The lake - which was watching them struggle - finally took pity on them.

'I'll come up to you!' the lake called out. 'But only if you give me something in return!'

'Anything!' the sisters cried.

'I want the most valuable thing you have!' said the lake.

So the youngest sister, who had a beautiful ring, took it off her finger, and threw it into the water down below.

And true to its word, the lake rose up.

THE SISTERS WERE OVERJOYED.

They filled all the pots that they had brought.

Just as they were about to turn back home, the youngest one started to cry.

'My ring! I want my ring back!'

Her sisters tried to reason with her.

'We have water in place of the ring!'

'We made a pact with the lake!'

But the youngest sister wouldn't listen.

'We have our water, now I want the ring back!'

She refused to go home. So there was nothing to do but to look for the ring...

...and the eldest sister stepped into the water.

SHE SEARCHED AND SEARCHED, BUT
THERE WAS NO SIGN OF THE RING.

'Come and help me!' she called out to her sisters
on the shore.

'It's dark in here and I can't see anything!'

So one by one, the others climbed into the
water, going deeper and deeper into the lake...
until... the water just swallowed them up.

From that day on, they were never seen again.

Some say they still live at the bottom of the
lake. It is said that the lake took them, for having
broken their promise.

WHY DID THIS STORY OCCUR TO ME NOW?

I think it's because we're afraid that our village will drown as well, like the sisters in the story. We are afraid of nature's fury.

I didn't fully understand what the story meant, as a child, and many things used to trouble me.

Why was the ring so important? Was it so bad of the youngest sister to want it back? Why did the lake - which was so kind to the sisters at first - let them drown?

I didn't like the way the story ended, and to comfort myself, I would imagine that they were all still living happily at the bottom of the lake.

THERE COULD BE ANOTHER REASON WHY THE STORY HAS COME TO ME NOW.

I think I understand its meaning.

We need nature - water, sun, air - to survive, but she doesn't really need us. She is generous to us, but she has some conditions, and we have to respect them.

The ring in the story stands for a bargain that the sisters made with the lake – a promise that they then broke. When you go against a bargain and become greedy, nature punishes you, like the lake did with the sisters. Her laws are very strict.

You can't exceed your limits, or take more than what is due to you.

DID WE TAKE MORE THAN OUR DUE?

As for as our village goes, I don't think so.

We have always been modest in our wants. We would like some development to secure our basic need for water, but not in any way that would harm the place in which we live. The story that my mother told me comes from people who have lived closely with nature, and are respectful of the give and take she requires.

No, the problem we are facing is not due to anything we've done – it has to do with the greed of the city. Not everyone in the city, but rich and powerful people who don't care about anything as long as they can get what they want.

SUCH PEOPLE HAVE TURNED THE CITY INTO
A MONSTER.

It is never satisfied, eating everything in its path.

And now our village is likely to get swallowed up by the
river as well, if this plan goes through.

We are not responsible for causing nature's fury, but it
is we who have to pay for it. It is unjust: this much is
clear to me, even though I don't have all the answers
to these huge problems.

All I can offer is the story of the sisters and the lake, to
urge people to think about keeping up our side of the
bargain with nature.

We thank the Cultural Institute of King's College, London
for supporting this project.

WATER
Copyright © 2018 Tara Books Private Limited
For the illustrations: Subhash Vyam
English text from the Hindi oral narrative
by Subhash Vyam: Gita Wolf

Design: Laura Nogueira

First printing: 2017

For this edition:
Tara Publishing Ltd., UK | www.tarabooks.com/uk
and
Tara Books Pvt. Ltd., India | www.tarabooks.com

Production: C. Arumugam
Printed in India by Canara Traders and Printers Pvt. Ltd.

ISBN: 978-93-83145-61-4